FOREVER GROWING

FOREVER GROWING

SOME NOTES ON A CREDO FOR TEACHERS

By PAUL GREEN

CHAPEL HILL
THE UNIVERSITY OF NORTH CAROLINA PRESS

Copyright, 1945, by
The University of North Carolina Press

FOREVER GROWING

I

LIFE IS LIKE A TREE FOREVER GROWING, AND MAN is part of that life. And though he must continue to be a man as long as he exists, still he has the power to become unlike himself and ruined and beastly if he will. Nothing is protected in its *status quo ante* against the possibilities of its own future and flux and undoing, neither man's God nor fate, nor man himself. Change is forever taking place, and there is no abiding of things as they are. In any particular thing or conglomerate of things every tomorrow, every minimuscule of time brings its process of differentiation and further varying. *Panta rei,* says the weeping philosopher.

But wherefore weep?

Panta rei, everything flows. And if the particulars, the conglomerates which make up the sum of the whole, are eternally changing, so is the whole which they constitute. Then where is permanence to be found beyond change? Where is truth with her verities to be sought for—if truth abides?

Permanence might be expected in a realm where impermanence does not appear. Naturally. We might find it in the opposite of these particulars, the whole of things perhaps. Now the opposite of things is nothings, or nothingness. But this is a state identical with the state of death—this opposite. Then it seems death is the permanence, the nothingness we seek. But does not death, this nothingness, also suffer change even as the particulars and conglomerates in life? It does.

Then there is no permanence in death. It too upboils and is activated. For life will not let it be. Life seizes upon the inert body-of-death, takes it apart piecemeal and speckmeal, plunders it, absorbs it, informs its ownself with new vitality from it, uses it as the flame uses the wood, as the body uses the blood, as the rain the cloud, and as the sap uses the flower or the tree. But is not the wood the source of flame, the body the source of the blood, the cloud of the rain, and the flower and the tree the source of the sap? That too.

Each owes it being to the other. And insofar as one is a separate being it is so through the vitalizing process of causation flowing in and between them.

Thus in this rich and mutual altruism life goes on. The inorganic feeds the organic, and the organic is everlastingly busy growing itself into full form, reproducing its kind, either better or worse in excellence and never the same, and giving its body into death in turn for the feeding and making of its kind that comes after it. The existence of one is the perpetuity of the other.

What humility! What sacrifice! And where is the secular loose talk about the law and the red dripping tooth and claw and the survival of the fittest, meaning the most cruel!

Well, it depends upon who is seeking for what and why and how as to the findings that result. For there is in nature a basic co-operativeness and beneficence which heals and helps even as a cool spring does a panting thirst, or love does desire and food does hunger. That too. And nature's children know it. And all youthful and healthy people who have not been contaminated and corroded by the fad of analysis and dead learning and the tools and methods of pragmatic insolence and pride—they know it well and feel it. And this co-operativeness, this beneficence, this changing activity of need and fulfillment, of life into death and death into life is a process— the process of creation.

A wise man said, "Except a corn of wheat fall into the ground and die, it abideth alone." And he also said, "Greater love hath no man than this that a man lay down his life for his friend." And another said, "How are the dead raised up? And with what body do they come? Thou foolish one, that which thou sowest is not quickened except it die." And still another said—a voice of antiquity, ever-vital and ever-creative and spilling out its enrichment and encouragement for man—this voice said—"And now abideth faith, hope, charity, these three; but the greatest of these is charity."

The world process is creative then, both as to particulars and as to the whole! That is the truth, that is the permanence we require.

2

But this is an old and obvious truth to us—or it should be. We have heard it from Samson and his riddle of the bees and the honey and the bones, from the weary wanderer and the riddle of the sphinx. We heard it from Plato in his metaphysic of mortality and immortality and darkness and light. Plotinus and Origen told us the same. And so did the great and learned Doctor of the thirteenth century, persuading us afresh to the freedom of the will, moral responsibility, intellectual love and the salvation of souls. And before him his own master Aristotle spoke out his intuition and seeing of the nature of virtue and the good life in a world of practical affairs.

And the same refrain was told to his love in later centuries by Petrarch, whom the scholars hold as "the first modern man" and who no doubt would have felt surprised and lonely in his century if he had known he was to be that. And before him was Dante with his epic of endurance and attainment, and before him Boethius. And later Erasmus, and the great Jew of Amsterdam, and the sickly Bacon, and much later the heavy plodding-footed Hegel and the healthful aristocratic Goethe—all said the same.

These and a thousand others like them have stood up along the path of literature and life and affirmed this truth. They have risen as living witnesses for the great process of creativeness, of life like a tree forever growing, or a mighty river forever flowing. But their words and their works have too often been in vain, most often have been in vain. We have not heard them.

3

For we teachers and scholars, caught in a scientific dispensation, find it impossible to accept life as a miracle of creativeness and growth. We are conditioned to believe that anything smacking of a miracle is perforce somehow mystic, medieval, sentimental, vaguely subjective and therefore unsound, not stopping to consider that the process of raising the question even is itself miraculous. It is the old scholasticism back again. And we fetch out our commonsense curricula and scientific methodologies and put them to bear upon the matter as if it were an object to be measured and described under a microscope.

And that's what we do—measure and describe, and set down findings. We categorize, catechize, cut up, analyze and compare and put appraisals upon the process of life and not only upon life but upon art and literature—which is worse. In place of life and art and literature, we thus substitute a method of derivation, matters of influence and style and types—whether of classic, romantic, realistic, naturalistic, expressionistic, or what not, and on down to as many adjectival examples of labeling as we can dig out of our inkwells or typewriters, being therefore the more solid and scientific in our results, we say.

4

And these labels we schoolmasters make and try to paste on the creative process of life are forever peeling off in the turn and twist and scouring of time. They will not stick. How could a label stick on a flowing river, or a stamp on shaking gay green leaves? But our activity continues. As soon as one label wears out or peels off or is blown away in contrary winds of doctrine or passes out of fashion, we have another and more scientific one ready for the pasting. And much of the frustration in purposes and hindrances to man's development and joy occurs because of this confusion of labels and names which we are responsible for. They are seals and deceptions stuck not so much perhaps on the body of the process of life and art itself as over the eyes of both the seeker and the seer.

Consider a term universally honored and respected by the schoolmen—to wit, nature's law. What confounding of wisdom and experience occurs in its name! A law of nature! The law! How it closes up the eyes of those who would look directly at the wonder and glory of the moon or the stars themselves but cannot see the object for the law which has it in thrall and makes it behave according to its will, the poor thing itself having no will. But there is in actual fact no law in nature, neither in the world of trees and men and growing things nor in the wheeling cindered stars. What we call the law is the way things act.

(But this sort of learning and mathematical formula-izing are understandable and necessary in the world of things—science. Through them we are "able to do business" with our environment. Through them the multitudinous phenomena of life around us are sifted out, catalogued, schematized and made amenable to the immediacy of our practical standards and needs. Thus science. But literature, art, life, are not sciences, not scientific. Still we keep on trying to deal with them as sciences, as "things" even.)

Natural law, then, is but a label or word-concept which we apply to change. It is a product of man's mind, an attribute he has given, a reading he has taken and made fast in the books. Things change. In order to change they have to change the way they do change or they could not change. Since they change the way they do change we say they change according to the law of change, a causal sequence in time and space, and these last are two more labels or word-concepts. The truth is they simply change. It is their nature to change, their creative nature. And rather than being beholden to any law, the law as we describe it is beholden to them. They *create* the law, self-create it. And potentially at any instant of "time" and any point in "space" an object may behave in a new creative way, a way it has never behaved before. It may even turn into its opposite nothing, or a nothing may suddenly become a thing —as is happening all the time. The process, then, varies in itself but it cannot behave "unlawfully," that is, contrary to itself.

This is the essential mystery of the universe which consciousness perceives and can wonder at and worship but which its understanding cannot penetrate and should not. For to do so consciousness would have to become other than itself, other than the process, which it can never do. Consciousness, awareness—which is identical with the process—cannot be conscious of its own cessation. And if the cessation of consciousness has ever been witnessed it has never known that fact, and the witness himself became the embodiment of that which was witnessed—as is well told in many books of the orient.

And between this awareness, this conscious mind, and the creative vital world, we educators place these misleading signs and tokens and distortions of meaning. And in doing so we are betraying our trust both as persons and as teachers; we betray our experience and its meaning for the future.

We are back at the old business of practicing the heresies of abstract medieval authority, except in this case the evil of abstraction is intensified. For we have made it of a lower scientific down-gazing earthly order, whereas in the old days of the wandering friar and hungry scurvy-bitten monk the gaze, however blinded, was upward and into a beneficent heaven.

5

We scholars and teachers are tough-hided sinners and good party members all right. We will do anything in the name of our creed or cause. We are propagandists of the veriest sort, and the hapless quivering body of truth is inquisitioned, quartered and drawn on any class or feast day. Look at the books we put out, the articles we print, our swarming midges of marginal footnotes, our journals, catalogues, compendia, our editions of volumes of art and volumes of literature, our floods of anthologies. And where is wisdom among them!

Everywhere we cut up life and the green creations of life into just such categories, movements, influences, currents, schools and the like, as mentioned above. And at any time we wish, we will reach and take a living artist, or a dead one, lift him from the fireside of his creative activity, place him on the shelf and catalogue him. And any student or seeker for wisdom and joy from this artist may come as if to an idol in a temple. But, shining big for him to see first of all, is a huge label or card or notice which proclaims this artist as of such and such a type—not just an artist, but a certain kind of artist. And the emphasis is always on the kind and not the art itself. And the pity is that, nearly every time, the label or card or notice gives life the lie. As time well proves. But the confused young neophyte does not find that out for many years after, maybe never. And he stays away from the temple.

And as with artists, so we do with other living souls whether they be preachers, politicians, or philosophers.

In a large and popular anthology of world literature now lying before me I noticed that Zola and Maupassant have been labeled in heavy letters as being in the category of the Naturalistic School—whatever that means. Apparently the editor is following along in dog-leash obedience with hundreds of other editors who have preceded him and uses several pages of *ad hoc* writing showing what is meant by naturalism and proving beyond a doubt and without rebuttal that these two authors, along with such others as Gorki and Dreiser, are condemned to this classification till the house of Belial freezes over and there's nothing to be done about it. Only as exponents and representatives, propagandists and exemplifiers of naturalism shall we know them.

I turn a wad of pages back in the same anthology and find that Aeschylus and Sophocles are representative of the classical period or school or age and nothing else. And from the editor's long and thorough essay on the nature of classicism, its balance and restraint, I am persuaded what vastly different creatures these four men were. In fact they were not four men. They were four propagandists—two for naturalism, two for classicism.

Again what a confusion of tongues we editors and scholars indulge in! Ah, these labels! Are there not blood and thunder and guts and organs of fecundity, liver and lights, tumors, thighs, stallions, procreation and abundant animal life, in the stately "classical" drama and in Homer's epics even as in the "naturalistic" Zola and Maupassant! Yes, plenty of them, plenty of "naturalism." In fact Aeschylus out-Zolas Zola. Open up the *Agamemnon* and read the scene where the wild and turbulent Cassandra sees the children of Thyestes sitting as gory phantoms above the doomed king's house. "See ye these infants sitting here on the palace like to phantoms of dreams?— Children just as if they had perished by the hands of their kinsmen—their hands crammed with the meat of their own entrails, a piteous mess, of which their father tasted."

Or take another of his plays, *The Eumenides,* and read the scene, for instance, in the interior of the temple of Apollo where we can see and hear the shuddering and grotesque and wild snaky-headed women, hear their whimpering moanings, their scaly raspy movements and see rising from the ground the ghost of murderous and murdered Clytemnestra smoking with blood. Or turn to the golden and symmetrical, classic Sophocles and read how Oedipus tears out his own eyes, after having killed his own father and married his own mother and begot four children, half-brothers and sisters to himself. And there, see, the tragic queen Jocasta hanging from a rafter by the neck dead of shame and grief!

And consider sad and mellow Euripides with all his murders and betrayals and gods in the machine, and the story of his hysterical bloody Medea, mother and killer of children, her own. And pick up Homer and read of his devastations and lust and blood, the spearing and letting out of brains, the defilement of Hector's body, the eating of the dead by dogs, the hate and treachery and cunning, the quarrels among the gods, the bickering of Aphrodite and Athena, and the god of war himself running with cowardly howls over the plain, and then the crafty double-dealing of Odysseus. And so on, and so on.

Yes, here are fervency and excess—both as to content *and* form!

6

When we forget our tokens and labels and signs and hierarchy of pigeon-holing and think of the works, the stories and plays and poems, themselves, we find that they are part of the creative process of life and men in life, and as such we can enjoy them, draw from them, be enriched and refreshed through them. Our learned findings of influences and kinds and types only get in the way and are a hindrance. They get between the appreciator and the object of his appreciation—that is, a really *felt* appreciation. And they are deadly for the creative artist. In fact a creative artist can learn only from a preceding work or art or master if he thinks of the painting as painting and the painter or poet as a creative spirit, a technician working at a job, never giving a hang as to what school or movement he might belong to. And what is true of the creative apprentice is just as true if not truer of the student and critic. And if it is true of these why is it not also true for us teachers and schoolmen?

For do we not all live by the same bread of life!

Even as I write out these words my daughter is downstairs doing a paper for her scholarly professor on "Coleridge as Romanticist." What of Coleridge as just—poet? Or what of Coleridge's poetry—just that—with all its magic and music and exquisite imagination and delicacy of tone and touch and thought? Why not have her write about them? And why ever any such label as "Romanticist" to bring her nearer to him when it puts him farther off? Why not just let him be, and let all the others be, and so let her receive them and their fire and glory and delight into her young soul? These should be the matter of interest, of concern and inspiration.

But instead she has to be, at the hard and blind and bull-headed behest of her professor, searching her young noggin for secondhand and unfelt words that will show she has surprised the secret out of the sage of Hampstead and henceforth will know the old, loquacious, metaphysical boy for what he is—not a spirit and a miraculous soul but a type, an example of a movement writ down by us schoolmen as romanticism. It may take her years to recover from this damage and wrong filling of her mind, this wrong teaching which dries up her emotions and sterilizes her dreams. She may get contaminated by this jargon of analyzing and "sciencizing" and go out as a teacher of literature herself and help contaminate others. She may never be able to approach Coleridge again, fresh and unprejudiced and pure as she should—approach him with an open heart in which the seeds and images of his beauty may thrillingly fall and as thrillingly grow. And so she will pass on to the next poet who stands in line as a representative of the movement, Wordsworth, and make the same tragic failure of missing the fragrance and breath of his glorious work, fail completely to feel the creative wonder of what he wrote, writing him down in emptiness the while—Romanticist.

7

I remember one lonely Sunday on the farm when I was a boy. The day before in town I had met up with a book-peddler and bought a copy of Shakespeare's *Hamlet*. And with the family gone off to church and the house silent and empty, I read the play. And as I read, I grew more interested and filled with suspense as to the people and their fate in the drama. And emotion became more and more packed up in me. And finally I came to the scene where poor piteous Ophelia enters with brains broken and mind deranged, speaking her little mad and anguished sayings—"There's rue for you, and here's some for me. We may call it herb of grace o' Sundays. O, you must wear your rue with a difference. There's a daisy. I would give you some violets, but they withered all when my father died. They say he made a good end." (Singing.) "For bonny sweet Robin is all my joy." And the tears gushed from my eyes, my heart opened with a yearning deep and wide.

> "O wert thou in the cauld blast,
>   On yonder lea, on yonder lea,
>   My plaidie to the angry airt,
>   I'd shelter thee, I'd shelter thee."

That day was a mark in my life. And because of that fresh, wild appreciation, untrammeled and unprepared for by any professorial coaching as to influences and types and methods by which the play might have been derived to represent the Elizabethan age or something other than itself—because of that, *Hamlet* has stood solidly by me, a rich storehouse through the years, and has meant more to me than it otherwise could possibly have meant. And Ophelia has continued to live her sweet and piteous life in the recesses of my soul.

Another lonely hot Sunday on the farm I was lying in my sweaty little shed room reading the Bible, when I came upon the twelfth chapter of *Ecclesiastes*. I suddenly sat up in delight at what I read—the beauty of it thrilled me and put a stuffiness in my throat. I hurried out of the room and down the side porch into the kitchen where my sister was getting lunch. "Listen, Mary," I said, "listen." And I read, "Or ever the silver cord be loosed, or the golden bowl be broken, or the pitcher be broken at the fountain or the wheel broken at the cistern."

"That's wonderful," she said. And she stood by the stove, holding a little piece of firewood balanced in her hand, her eyes wide and thoughtful as she went on hearing the words over a second time in her mind. "Read it again," she said. And I did, and for a while we shared the beauty and wonder of those lines and others in the chapter. And because of that experience, *Ecclesiastes* has always remained one of my favorite books. I thank my stars that I was not "prepared" for it by the usual teacher, say, of Comparative Literature, who talked of a preceding Stoic philosophy and currents of Hebraic pessimism which brought the book to being—a resultant of clearly demarked and discernible scholarly laws and forces. For it would have been marred before I got to it—as so many of the great works of literature were marred for me in precisely that way.

I

But forget books a while and look about at life—at life before and now and after.

Put a question to that old hoary figure Paul Bunyan—he who dug out the Great Lakes the year the blue snow fell and turned itself into ink, who combed his beard with a scraggly pine tree and whose mighty big Babe ox had a horn spread of a day's crow-flight from tip to tip.

Or make speech with that great fighter Davy Crockett who swallowed a thunderbolt from heaven—that time he had his mouth open making a political speech in a thunderstorm. And the thunderbolt never hurt him—soured his stomach a bit, but that was all.

Wake up, wake up, brother! Day's a-breaking, snakes a-waking, and creation is at work.

Aw, go away, child.

Yeh, did. And he went home with a piece of the sunrise in his pocket.

Or walk out, way out and wide and consult with John Henry the Negro muscle man who led the last fierce fight between man and the machine and lost his life in the battle but who now lives on in the minds of every lover of Negro folklore.

What is that noise we hear, Mammy, like timber crackling yonder?

That's John Henry's hammer, chillun, John Henry's nine-pound hammer falling in the sky.

Or go have talk with Mike Fink the fighter, or Stackolee the bad man, or Roy Bean, or Buffalo Bill, or Casey Jones, or gentle and earth-blessing Johnny Appleseed, or the Arkansas Traveler, or even the prideful prancing Br'er Rabbit.

Or make a query of red-headed Thomas Jefferson where he watches on Monticello Hill, or of George Washington muffled and eternal behind his ivied tomb, or Lincoln marbled and profound and guarded beneath his columns there on Potomac River.

They all speak up with one affirming voice of creation and work, denying all weakness and chances gone. They proclaim that we are a thundering mighty nation of people and up to thundering and mighty things both collectively and individually and we must take care that we never be up to anything else.

And there is no time for confusion, frustration, and despair.

(And why do I not say, go talk, yes, have converse with the professors and teachers in this land, the keepers of wisdom and inspiration and the holy grail of youth? Why not? Because it is written that the son who asks for bread should not be handed a stone.)

Geographically, industrially, meteorologically, sociologically, we are one of the most active, yeasty and turmoiling regions of the earth, and vastness, power and daring reach are our middle name. Yes, they tell us just that, these names, these persons, these characters, and life itself about us tells us that. Loudly they all tell it, and I believe it.

One of Britain's austere and historical deans said recently that the United States might not be the loveliest nation of the globe but he found it the most exciting.

Well as for loveliness too, as well as power, there are many definitions, descriptions and names.

2

Once in a burned-out region of Tennessee, amid sulphur fumes, smoking slag heaps and desolation I saw a native leaning against his cabin door watching the evening sun go down. And the scene around him was illumined in a kind of hellish glory. He shook his head at it all and said, "I jest couldn't feel at home anywhere else, it's so purty here." And beautiful it was to him and that in spite of the fact that a WPA welfare worker was at the moment trying to persuade him to learn to wear shoes and go to the movies to see Lana Turner—in order that his soul might be lifted up and his social betterment assured.

Praise God from whom all blessings flow!

But still in passing I plead that this native son be allowed to stay where he is, unhelped by sprout of grass or bird or living tree though he be, yet even so finding his life of beauty-in-ugliness sufficient to the day thereof.

A genial and mystic poet from Ireland once told me he found our country too huge and raw and dynamic and unhumanized for his comfort and praise. He couldn't feel close and warm to it, couldn't take it to his bosom's love and appreciation the way he could the little byways, bogs, and lanes of Ireland. And beauty is only to be found, he said, where one can cherish the object, feel and know the sources and tokens of beauty, can endow them or depict them with his own imagination, can know and sense them closely and intimately. One square mile of soil he found preëminently beautiful and loved it in accordance with its beauty. And why not? "For," said he, "I've painted every square yard of it there in Ireland." The distances here he found too great, too much wild and uprooted life and piled stumps and entrails of earth showing, too much of time's riches going to waste—from the thundering and fire-bitten forests of the northwest to the vast gut of New York City spewing its sewage and human refuse into the cavernous depths of the Atlantic Ocean.

He found the American citizens rushing hither and yon over these vast distances between two oceans, harnessing and conquering and building and trading—whether in turbines, soap, leather, gewgaws, panties, jewsharps, or chewing gum. And always the challenge was to shape, to fashion, to create—always a too keen and overflooding challenge, he said. Here were rivers still to be dredged, jetties to be made, and ever the viaducts and cables reaching, and bridges and mighty cranes lifting and gouging and dumping their load, as man harnessed nature and her things to his will and purpose.

One morning this poet awoke in New Orleans, he recounted, and looking out of his window he gazed upon the flat fog-shrouded Mississippi. What an uncouth, wild, and barbaric name after all! And showing up like black primeval fish seeking air the grimy wet snags of stumps and trees protruded menacingly through the fog. A nightmarish and maleficent nature unloosed! And it oppressed him to think that the river stretched far away through limitless mud and prairie grass to the Great Lakes to the north, lying huge and uncouth like a weighty serpent across a continent.

And everywhere power, strength, spilling richness and ugliness. And there was no time for meditation, he said.

3

Well, as for meditation also there are many definitions and names. There is the yogi kind of sitting on a slitting wire between two trees or the cross-legged kind in which the sinews and kidneys and powers of a man gradually dry up as he sits with empty birds' nests in his hair contemplating the vacuous and vasty finitude. Then there is the active, spear-pointed, dynamic kind that guides a project forward—the lantern of practical intent that illuminates the will, that travels like a righteous judgment and a forming power even inside and out the deed.

True, we have too often lost the meditation, the contemplative process in the practical splurge of doing things—of trading and barter—being busy and creating a pother of theories and new-fangled creeds in addition, such as the fad for psychiatry, subjective psychology, and vitamins, when more thoughtfulness and less frenzy would have been better by every test. But we are a building, a pioneer, creative nation mainly, delighting in enormous turnovers of goods, services, and ever new enterprises, and immediacy is sometimes overpowering.

And even so the joy, the delight, the emotions of this creativeness we have celebrated in our arts. In our folk arts we have at least, and in our sophisticated ones we should.

And we will.

For here to our hand, with the possible leisure which ever more and more perfect machines are providing for us, is the chance to create a culture the like of which has occurred perhaps only a few times in the history of the world—once in China, once in India, once in Palestine perhaps, once in Greece, and once in England. And only by the glory of its thoughts, its ideals, its imagination is a nation or an age finally great. And if we work for this, then the worldwide co-operation which man is dying to bring about, in this present conflict, for us the living will be that much nearer a fact, and the ancient and grand illusion of *"dulce et decorum est pro patria mori"* will not be practiced with such anguish to all concerned.

And we are working more and more for it.

For instance, the schools are taking up the native American music. More and more our young composers are using the lyrical material of our fields, and hills, and mines, and factories, and halls. Our dramatists are going to the basic and active imaginative life of the people for their subject matter. And the same is true of our poets, painters, and crafters. And someday, who knows—we may be able to set the green-growing joy of our dreams and our arts up in the full sunlight of economic favor.

And it is high time already.

For now the frontier is over for us—the spatial, horizontal frontier in which we formerly were wont to extend our restless personalities. The last golden yard of California has been explored—we have come to a definite sense of our neighbors, south and north and of the oceans on either side. This is as it should be. Ahead in time not space is the period of intensification—of a smelting, of a processing, and distributing the stuff of our nation—of learning to know and express ourselves from within and not by the dull and witless aping of authority, of ill-conceived and second-hand commandments. And that means first of all that we should know and appreciate our tradition, our past. And knowing it, appreciating it, means using it in a vital creative way—the way of art.

This we teachers must somehow learn and we must tell it to others.

4

Three hundred years ago the dreamers came into this land of ours—the rabble, the crooks, the cranks, the weak men, the idealists, the strong men, the hopeful and despairing—and all were hunting for something, something not only outside themselves but inside.

First they conquered the wilderness.

Second they created the democratic form of government.

Third, they led the way in the creation of the machine age.

It took them two hundred and fifty years to do these three things. My contention is, to repeat, that now it is up to us to do the fourth thing, to create an age of culture in the life of our country—(yes, I know that's a suspect word, but still it is the right word)—the age of art, true science, right thinking—the transfiguration of our life into terms of art, the art of living. It seems to me that one might say that it was for this very thing that our country was created. And if we fail to make our complete contribution in bringing it to pass, just so much we fail those who struggled before us, fail the hopes and the purpose of those who come after us, and worst of all fail and betray ourselves, ourselves as both human beings and teachers.

We are already fifty years late!

5

Yes, that's what I mean—life as an art:—green winter fields even to the lyric, lazy, and indulgent South; paint on the houses, flowers at the door, and care and beauty and love surrounding our bare, pitiful little country schools and churches; lights and water and conveniences for men and their housewives, not that they may snooze the light away and grow fat in greasy ease, but that they may have more time for books and music and drama and singing. And then outdoor plays and festivals and the beauty of maydays and the sweet and tender girl queen with the prideful young king walking by her side, and good health and joy and imagination among our children, and throughout the land a people alive with the sense of celebration—celebration of their past, their present, and their future—with festivals and choruses and orchestras and all the folk arts flourishing for the mutual stimulation and give and take among us everyone! For these are the decorations of life, the inspiration, the fire, and color and drive and depthful meaning of life. And it is now no longer a matter of the pocketbook and gadgets of commerce, if it ever was, but a matter of the soul. It is the soul I'm talking about.

I am talking about the soul.

6

And what is this soul? Yours and mine? I ask myself this question, and I try to answer it. It is the self, ourself. And it has its leanings and its drawing-back, its yearnings and its urges, its monitors and guides.

The soul is the most elemental factor of human life since it is the self. There are three moods or phases of this soul or self in relation to the outside world—cognition (awareness), emotion (feeling), and action (doing). And each and all are of infinite variety.

There are also, according to certain oriental psychologists, three moods or phases of the self in relation to the self—self-consciousness, self-feeling, and self-assertion. And these three also are infinite in their meanings and relationships.

The two primary guides of the self—and by primary I mean first and instinctive—through these phases of life are pleasure and pain (joy and sorrow, happiness and misery, gladness and sadness, and so on). And just as the self or soul cannot be analyzed further, so pleasure and pain cannot be further analyzed, even though they may be described and causally derived by logic. For they precede any process or method of analysis at any moment. And all such analysis is obviated in the very nature of the act of experiencing, of trying to understand.

Then it follows that we like what pleases us and dislike what pains us. On the one hand we wish to take in, to absorb, to embrace, to have more of. And on the other hand we wish to push away, to repel, to avoid, and to have less of.

On the one hand we love, and on the other we hate.

7

Now love works for unity and identity among all selves or souls. Hate works for disunity and disparity of all selves. Love seeks to unite, hate seeks to separate.

(No doubt some sort of categorical arrangement could be worked out for the different expressions of love and hate or pleasure and pain. And some philosophers have done so—as for instance—

Attraction plus the consciousness of the equality with one's self of the attractive object is affection or love proper—

Attraction plus the consciousness of the superiority to one's self of the attractive object is reverence—

Attraction plus the consciousness of the inferiority

to one's self of the attractive object is benevolence;—or—

Repulsion plus the consciousness of the difference from one's self of the repulsive object is hate or aversion proper—

Repulsion plus the consciousness of the equality of the object of repulsion is anger—

Repulsion plus the consciousness of the superiority of the object of repulsion is fear—

And so on to whatever conclusion of labeling we academes may desire.)

And as biological human love is not compatible with complete identification with the object of its love except in the *production* of another self (child), so neither is hate compatible with total suppression, disparity and separation except in the *destruction* of another self (enemy).

And the same is true on a higher level. For love is creative not only biologically but spiritually, and hate is destructive not only spiritually but biologically. And just as love works endlessly for creation and beauty and light, so does hate work endlessly for death, destruction and darkness. (The eastern philosopher tells us how in war the destroyed enemy still lives with the conqueror—still haunts him, remains with him in monuments, special days, speeches, and pledges and oaths of immolation. The slayer is also the slain, and "he whom I gave unto death was handed back to me in the immortality of the event.")

Love then is the highest reason.

Hate is ignorance in its worst form. And this is true at all times, whether in peace or war, in plenty or famine.

8

Now the beautiful is that which incites and excites love. I mean the truly beautiful.

There is no set or formal measurement or apt standard of beauty, thank God, for it varies with taste and time. But it never varies as to its inner power of giving pleasure to human beings, of giving true happiness.

Speech alive is poetry. And the more alive it is the more poetic richness is in it.

Words so alive have the power to stir up, to move, to inspire in the reader the emotions with which they themselves are alive. And this gives pleasure.

(What is said of poetry is true of the other arts, the difference being only in the terminology proper to each.)

This receiving of pleasure is a process in appreciation, an imaginative one. And art and poetry and literature are like chalices and abounding springs which hold life essentialized for the tasting and drinking and enjoyment as one feels and finds the need to so taste and drink. They are means of storing up the joy and richness of experience against the leakage and waste of time.

(Let us always remember that this intensification of beauty into art is nothing more than the enhancement, the intensification of the consciousness of beauty which is general and as far-reaching as mankind itself. And oh that man might realize this glory, this divine gift and talent which he possesses! And woe to him when he does not, for the rust of battle shall consume his bones, and the timbers of his temples and market-places shall fall upon him with a great thunder!)

Now in regard to the cruel, the disgusting, the fearful, and other such kindred subjects, why is art pleasing which deals with them? The answer is that in the treatment their "ugliness" disappears and they become sublimated and idealized with the emotion and intent of the artist who interpreted them. We view them as representatives of actuality and not as actuality itself. And the emotions and ideas aroused in us by the contemplation of these examples of art fill us and increase the abundance of our personality and are therefore pleasurable.

How is it possible to get pleasure out of witnessing or reading a tragedy, for instance? The answer seems simple, and is simple. For the spectator or reader is stirred to sympathy and pity for the tragic sufferer *in whom he has grown interested,* and a feeling of benevolence is aroused in him. And therefore the quality of mercy is doubly blessed.

The joy of sympathizing, of self-sacrifice, of giving unto another is pleasurable, pleasurable to the deeper and more spiritual self and is only unpleasurable to the shallower, more physical, less spiritual self.

Again, the urge to associate with, to help the suffering one, to lift him up, to ease him, brings with it not only the feeling but often the very picture or pictures of the completed association, and therefore a gained fullness of personality in this giving out results. Accordingly the feeling is pleasurable.

In tragedy, then, man's benevolent and unselfish self is called more strongly into play than not. And in giving, potentially and imaginatively (and rarely actually or factually) he the spectator the more completes himself therein and within. For such giving is born of love.

For love gives and hate takes away. Tragedy, then, arouses love. And the pleasure resulting therefrom is not a selfish or fearsome one at all—as Aristotle would seem to have us believe. In fact, the purgation or purifying he speaks of comes, and I think can only come, through this very unselfishness of giving, this love that loves to give.

This is a truth that lies at the center of man's interpretation of the universe.

9

And what of this universe? What do we believe about it? What does it mean to us? (I ask myself these things also and I try to answer them.)

Well, I believe in it and its heaven and earth as uncreated, everlasting, without beginning or end. (I say uncreated—insofar as having a beginning, but continuously self-creative insofar as it continues to endure.) I consider it as the totality of matter or energy that is.

I believe in life which inhabits and uses this totality of matter either partially or wholly or anywhen—which was created, had a beginning in consciousness and shall have an end.

Both matter and life are forever changing—always have been, always will be (speaking of life while it exists), but the identity of their change is in name only, for matter changes helplessly, self-helplessly and blindly, and life changes for a purpose.

The fact of the creation of life, the appearance of life in this material universe was miraculous and precedent to any purpose except its own creation, but once created it was all purpose, and when it lacks purpose for long it disappears, and the matter which once contributed to it—its body—returns again to the blind totality of matter to be used by other life and lives in other spaces and other times perchance.

To repeat, this space and time we speak of are not real in themselves—they are only words, label-concepts of description of change. There is neither space nor time apart from matter and life. Space applies to matter and time applies to life. There is no empty space and no dead time except as life is dead.

Then we have matter and living matter—or matter alive—the inorganic and the organic in familiar terms. And the organic is of a higher order than the inorganic, just as light is of a higher order than darkness. And one might say that the reason for darkness is to affirm the light. So evil—what we call evil—might be thought of to exist only to affirm the good. Just as the only reality for hate is as it exists to help affirm its opposite, love.

Now life seems to be of three different orders, not only seems but is—the vegetable, the animal, and man. The animal is higher than the vegetable, and man higher than the two.

By higher I mean of consciousness and meaningful purpose.

I said matter has no purpose and that life once it is life is filled with purpose. What is that purpose? Excellence in itself. And what is excellence?

It is the making more and more manifest through whatever means—conscious or unconscious—whether through thinking, willing, feeling and doing or whatever else—the ideal nature (the bent, intent, trend) of the living thing or animal or person concerned.

The excellence of a tree depends on how fine a tree it is and becomes. The excellence of an animal the same. The excellence of a man the same.

The first two—the vegetable and the animal—have no conscious means of working towards that end—that excellence. Therefore, they are sinless, never triumphant, never shamed, and are beholden to no moral law. In them the power of change is all-powerful. They are helpless in its grip—that is, helpless in the grip of their own living organic nature, a condition which could not be otherwise. Now man has a conscious means of working towards his own excellence—himself, his self, the soul. In fact the self or soul gives him his drive, his inspiration, the meaning of his life—to develop and improve himself and his world in beauty about him. That is, in brief, man as a self is a spirit.

By the word spirit or spiritual I mean—in and for and by itself in terms of an ideal of perfection.

Then is perfection attainable? No. And it should not be—(and notice the word "should" never occurs in the plant and animal realm. That is the point too, not collateral but corroborative)—for two reasons. First, change continues, and no change in perfection is possible except to imperfection. Second, the nature of the perfecting process is creation and growth in and towards the ideal, and beyond perfection there can be neither. So man cannot reach perfection, but the perfecting of himself in his art, his things, his hopes, his dreams, his deeds, his loves is his continuous privilege and duty.

Perfection lies in the struggle to reach perfection.

10

So whether as a creature man came into being, into existence by design or accident, whether he shall likewise disappear or not are not his real concern. That concern is with his own living present self, his present world, and his present fellows. (And in this I include responsibility to the future, of course, though not to the past, obviously.) These latter he can do something about. The past is beyond him except in the main as it may be memorialized.

Nor need he bother about why he is endowed with a spirit. Such a question is unreal and cannot be answered—any more than there can be a final answer to the final question about the reality (nature) of matter. The actual fact has to be accepted and business carried on from there, for, to repeat, the nature of first awareness is such acceptance. Suffice it then that man is a spirit and that he seek to live as a spirit.

Thus we find our time-space-change-law universe or universes energized with these phenomena—— completed in them and infused with them:

>Matter
>Life
>Spirit

Matter is purposeless.
Life is practically purposeful and necessitous.
Spirit is ideally purposeful and free.

Between the first and the second is the mysterious linkage of consciousness, of awareness.

Between the second and the third is a man's soul, his sense of responsibility, his ethical sense, and the consciousness of free will. And this sense is incorporative of the preceding linkage of awareness. It is man's real self.

What is consciousness? The principle of awareness. It is quantitative.

What is the self? The principle of appreciation. It is qualitative.

And as the former can feed and enter into the second, so can the second become spiritual—or not.

So now begins the problem of man's ritual and curriculum towards that higher ideal of the spirit, that ideal and *art*. And here the trouble lies both for him and for the teacher.

II

What, then, is the answer? What should a teacher teach? How should he approach the subject?

Why, teach the subject itself, approach the subject itself, approach the subject directly and not put up labels and curtains that stand opaque and dividing between the seer and the seen. Get the student close to the object of his interest. Let him work at it too. Let him try his hand in practice. Let him experience the poem, or whatever it is, in the raw, in its natural wonder. Goethe says wisely enough, "He who does not take an active part in certain subjects knows them but half and superficially." And again in his *Conversations,* "A thing requires not only to be read and studied but to be done"—that is, done wherever one can. And there should be as little separation between creation and appreciation, between theory and practice as possible.

Some time ago a young actor was at my house trying out for a part in a play. The part he was interested in was that of a young pioneer woodsman. This actor was from the heart of New York and knew practically nothing of what a pioneer's life might consist of. The character in the play was supposed to be a hefty worker with an axe, and the soft-handed Brooklynite in reading the part showed that for all his two hundred pounds of hulk he didn't know what the feel of an axe was nor what the young pioneer really meant when the dialogue spoke of "cutting trees and clearing land and sweating with the joy of it." So I took him out into my woods for a while to cut trees, still talking the play. We cut and chopped and cut some more. Soon our coats were off, then our shirts, then our undershirts. And the sweat poured. The actor puffed and blew. In an hour or two his hands were blistered. But he liked it. And through these blisters something of the character's character entered into his body and spirit. And when we returned to the living-room after supper to go on with the reading, he read with a real and glowing difference.

And so it goes.

And we can only know and love what we grow interested in, what we work at.

There are the three principles of knowing and feeling and doing, and they all become one most completely in the doing.

12

And here is this planet we call the earth, the wise man said. Its soil has been tilled for untold millenniums and yet its strength is not exhausted, nor will it be exhausted. Its generative and procreative powers remain undiminished. Treat it creatively, give it a little rain, a little sun, and spring and summer and teeming autumn with all their fruits and beauties will pour themselves into the air again. So it is with man as with the earth.

For he is a quickened spirit, a self. He is neither scientist, pharisee, homo sapiens, classicist, romanticist, animal, nor humanist. He is a self, a living being, a personality, a soul. And he has his visions, his freedom of will and his ideals accordingly, and his essential nature is creativeness. There is in him a primal impulse and impetus towards the making of a truly beautiful and vital world. And however obscured, hindered, detoured by false doctrines and prophets, he will continue to strive towards that goal. But he needs help and that is the purpose of all teaching—to help him and help him creatively.... This is my credo.

13

And through the blue depths of the sky the bird flies, but the tips of its wings are never stained in it. Moreover it is written—that with faith a man thinks. Faithless he cannot think. And he who worships God as the great King milks heaven and drinks it day by day. His food is never exhausted...."And he shall be like a tree planted by the rivers of water, that bringeth forth his fruit in his season; his leaf also shall not wither, and whatsoever he doeth shall prosper."

For life is like a tree forever growing!

www.ingramcontent.com/pod-product-compliance
Lightning Source LLC
Chambersburg PA
CBHW031715230426
43668CB00006B/225